CW00617764

TEATIME TREATS

with illustrations by
HELEN ALLINGHAM RWS

FAVOURITE HOME-MADE CAKES

SALMON

Index

The "COUNTRY FARE" Series
COUNTRY FARE, TEATIME TREATS, TASTE OF SUMMER
Published by J Salmon Limited, 100 London Road, Sevenoaks, Kent TN13 1BB
First Edition 1994. Copyright © 1994 J Salmon Ltd.
Designed by The Salmon Studio. ISBN 1 898435 16 5

Printed in England by J Salmon Limited, Tubs Hill Works, Sevenoaks, Kent.

Banana Cake

9 oz. self-raising flour
10 oz. sugar
4 oz. margarine, softened
3–4 ripe bananas, mashed
2 eggs
½ teaspoon salt
1 teaspoon vanilla essence
½ teaspoon bicarbonate
of soda

FILLING
Jam, to choice
Whipped cream

Set oven to 375°F or Mark 5. Grease and line two 9 inch sandwich tins. This cake is best made in a food mixer. Put all the ingredients, except the bananas, together into the mixer bowl and mix on medium speed. When blended stir in the well-mashed bananas. Turn into the two tins and bake for 25–30 minutes. Turn out on to a wire rack to cool. When cool sandwich together with jam and whipped cream. Alternatively this cake can be served plain.

TIG BRIDGE

Saffron Buns

½ teaspoon saffron strands
1 lb. strong white flour
Pinch of salt
3 oz. butter
3 oz. currants or sultanas
1 oz. chopped candied peel
2 oz. sugar

½ oz. fresh yeast
1 teaspoon sugar
¼ pint warm milk

Soak the saffon strands in a little water overnight. Mix the flour and salt together in a bowl, then rub in the butter. Stir in the currants or sultanas, the peel and the 2 oz. of sugar. Stir the yeast and the 1 teaspoon of sugar into the warm milk. Make a 'well' in the dry ingredients, then pour in the yeast liquid. Strain the yellow saffron water into the 'well' and mix thoroughly to form a soft dough. Cover and leave in a warm place until the dough has doubled in bulk; this can take around 1 hour. Turn out on to a lightly floured surface and knead well. Shape into buns, about the size of Hot Cross Buns and set well apart on a greased baking sheet; leave to prove for about 20 to 30 minutes. Set oven to 425°F or Mark 7. Bake the buns for 10 to 15 minutes. Remove from the oven and brush the tops with a glaze made with 1 tablespoon sugar dissolved in a little warm milk, then return to the oven for 1 to 2 minutes. Serve hot, plain or with butter.

Apple Scones

8 oz. wholemeal self-raising flour

1 teaspoon ground cinnamon

1 teaspoon baking powder

4 oz. butter

2 oz. soft brown sugar

2 medium sized cooking apples, peeled, cored and finely diced

1 medium egg

Set oven to 375°F or Mark 5. Mix the dry ingredients together in a large bowl. Rub in the butter, stir in the sugar and the diced apple and lastly stir in the egg. Mould the mixture into 10 or 12 heaps (as you would for rock buns) and place on a floured baking tray. Bake for 20–25 minutes. Cool slightly before transferring to a wire rack. Serve split, with butter.

Iced Fruit Gingerbread

1 lb. flour
3 oz. sultanas
4 fl. oz. milk
6 oz. butter or margarine
6 oz. black treacle
6 oz. golden syrup
1 round teaspoon bicarbonate of soda
Pinch of salt
2 eggs, beaten
4 oz. caster sugar
1 teaspoon ground ginger

Set oven to 350°F or Mark 4. Grease and line a 7 inch square cake tin. Melt the butter, treacle, syrup and sugar gently in a saucepan. Sift the flour, ginger and bicarbonate of soda into a bowl. Add the salt and sultanas. Beat the eggs in a separate bowl, add the milk and then add to the flour mixture. To this add the warmed treacle mixture and mix well. Pour into the tin and bake for 45–60 minutes until firm. Cool on a wire rack. Ice with glacé icing. This cake may also be eaten plain.

ICING
8 oz. icing sugar
1 tablespoon water
1 tablespoon warmed golden syrup
Crystallised ginger for decoration

Icing: Add the warmed syrup to the sifted icing sugar. If too thick, add warm water carefully until a dropping consistency is achieved. Decorate with pieces of ginger.

Chocolate Eclairs

¼ pint water
1 oz. margarine
Pinch of salt
2½ oz. flour
2 small eggs
A few drops vanilla essence
Whipped cream
Chocolate glacé icing

Set oven to 450°F or Mark 8. Grease baking trays. Put the water, margarine and salt into a saucepan and bring to the boil. Remove from the heat and add the sifted flour, beating well. Return to the heat and cook gently until the mixture leaves the sides of the pan clean. Remove from the heat, add the essence and beat in the eggs one at a time. Pipe the mixture on to the baking trays, using a plain vegetable pipe (the size of the eclairs depends on personal preference). Bake for 25–30 minutes. When cold, split and fill with whipped cream and coat with chocolate glacé icing.

SPRING AT CHIDDINGFOLD

Shortbread

4 oz. butter
2 oz. caster sugar
6 oz. flour
2 oz. ground rice

Set oven to 350°F or Mark 4. Cream the butter and the sugar together in a bowl. Gradually sift in the flour and the ground rice, kneading the mixture into a ball. Roll or pat the dough on a floured surface into a round, about ½ inch thick. Place on a plain baking sheet. Pinch up the edges and prick the top with a fork. Bake for about 35–40 minutes or until firm and pale golden. While still warm, cut into triangles and sprinkle with caster sugar.

Boiled Fruit Cake

4 oz. margarine
4 oz. soft brown sugar
8 oz. mixed dried fruit
¼ pt water
9 oz. self-raising flour
1 egg, beaten
½ teaspoon salt
1 level teaspoon mixed spice

Put the margarine, sugar, dried fruit and water into a saucepan, bring slowly to the boil and simmer for 5 minutes. Allow to cool. Set oven to 325°F or Mark 3. Grease and line a 7 inch cake tin. Put all the remaining ingredients into a bowl, add the cooled fruit mixture and mix to a thick batter. Place in the tin and bake for 1½ hours or until a skewer inserted into the cake comes out clean. Leave to cool in the tin for 10–15 minutes and turn out on to a wire rack.

APPLE AND PEAR BLOSSOM

Walnut Bread

10 oz. self-raising flour
4 oz. caster sugar
4 oz. chopped walnuts
½ teaspoon salt
1 medium egg, beaten
7 fl. oz. milk

Grease a 2 lb. loaf tin. Mix all the dry ingredients together in a bowl. Add the beaten egg and the milk and mix thoroughly. Set aside for 20 minutes. Set oven to 325°F or Mark 3. Put the mixture into the tin and bake for 1–1¼ hours until risen and golden brown and a skewer inserted into the loaf comes out clean. Turn out on to a wire rack and when cold cut into thin slices and serve spread with butter.

Fruit Buns

12 oz. flour
4 oz. ground rice
2 teaspoons baking powder
4 oz. butter
3 oz. sugar
3 oz. currants
2 eggs, beaten
Milk

Set oven to 400°F or Mark 6. Mix the flour, ground rice and baking powder together in a bowl. Rub in the butter until the mixture resembles fine breadcrumbs, then stir in the sugar and currants. Mix in the eggs and sufficient milk to make a smooth firm paste. Turn out on to a lightly floured surface and roll out to 1 inch in thickness. Cut into 2 inch rounds and place on a greased baking sheet. Bake for 15 to 20 minutes until golden.

Seed Cake

6 oz. soft margarine
6 oz. caster sugar
3 eggs, separated
8 oz. self-raising flour
1 dessertspoon caraway seeds
A few drops of almond essence
Milk to mix

Set oven to 350°F or Mark 4. Grease and line a 7 inch cake tin. Beat the margarine and sugar together in a bowl until fluffy. Separate the yolks from the whites of the eggs and whisk the whites to form peaks. Beat the yolks. Add the whites to the creamed mixture and then add the yolks. Sprinkle in the caraway seeds and fold in the flour alternately, a little at a time, adding the almond essence. Add sufficient milk, as necessary, to form a thick batter. Put into the tin and sprinkle a few caraway seeds over the top of the mixture. Bake for 1 hour until well risen and until a skewer inserted into the cake comes out clean. Leave to cool for 10–15 minutes and turn out on to a wire rack.

Chocolate Cake

6 oz. soft margarine
6 oz. sugar
3 eggs, beaten
7 oz. self-raising flour
1 oz. cocoa powder
1 level teaspoon baking powder
Pinch of salt
1 tablespoon milk

Set oven to 375°F or Mark 5. Grease and line two 9 inch sandwich tins. Beat the fat and sugar together in a bowl until creamy. Add the beaten eggs and the sieved flour, baking powder, salt and cocoa. Add the milk and mix well to a soft dropping consistency. Divide the mixture into the tins and bake for 20 minutes. Turn on to a wire rack. When cool, sandwich together and also top with chocolate butter icing.

THE FISH-SHOP, HASLEMERE

Drop Scones

8 oz. self-raising flour
½ teaspoon salt
1 level tablespoon caster sugar
1 large egg
½ pint milk

Place the flour, salt and sugar into a bowl. Make a well in the centre and add the egg and the milk gradually, stirring to make a smooth, thick batter. Drop the mixture in tablespoons on to a hot, lightly greased griddle or heavy based frying pan. Keep the griddle at a steady, moderate heat and after 2–3 minutes when bubbles show on the surface of the scones, turn over and cook for 2 more minutes. Place the finished scones in a warm, folded tea towel; this will keep them warm and by keeping in the steam will prevent them from drying out. Serve warm with butter and jam or honey.

Walnut Cakes

4 oz. walnuts
1 egg white
1 tablespoon self-raising flour
4 oz. caster sugar
1 teaspoon orange flower water
Extra walnuts to decorate

Set oven to 375°F or Mark 5. Pound the 4 oz. of walnuts in a mortar or electric grinder until well ground. Beat the egg white in a bowl until stiff. Then add the sugar and beat until thick. Beat in the flour, walnuts and orange water until well mixed. Put separate teaspoonfuls of the mixture on to a greased baking tray and place a walnut in the centre of each. Bake for approximately 10–15 minutes until pale brown.

AN OLD BUCKINGHAMSHIRE HOUSE

Harvest Cake

8 oz. flour
8 oz. barley flour
1½ teaspoons baking powder
Pinch of salt
4 oz. sugar
4 oz. butter, softened
2 teaspoons golden syrup
½ pint milk
8 oz. sultanas

Barley flour can be bought from some health food shops but, if preferred, all plain flour can be used, though this will alter the taste somewhat.

Set oven to 350°F or Mark 4. Grease and line a 7 inch cake tin. Sieve the flour and barley flour together with the baking powder and salt. Cream the sugar and butter together in a mixing bowl, then stir in the syrup. Add the flours and the milk alternately to the creamed syrup mixture, combining well between each addition, and then fold in the sultanas. Turn the mixture into the tin and bake for 1½ hours or until a skewer inserted into the cake comes out clean. If the top appears to be browning too quickly, cover with a piece of foil. Cool in the tin for 10 to 15 minutes, then turn out on to a wire rack.

Bath Buns

1 lb. strong white flour
½ teaspoon salt
2 oz. butter
2 oz. caster sugar
4 oz. sultanas
2 oz. chopped mixed peel
1 oz. fresh yeast
½ pint tepid milk
2 medium eggs, beaten

TOPPING
2 oz. coarse sugar
1 egg, beaten

Put the flour and salt into a large bowl and rub in the butter. Stir in the sugar, sultanas and mixed peel. Blend the yeast with a little of the tepid milk to a smooth cream. Make a well in the centre of the flour and add the yeast liquid, the beaten eggs and remaining milk and mix to a soft dough. Knead on a lightly floured surface until smooth. Place in a clean bowl, cover with a damp cloth and leave to rise in a warm place until double in size. Re-knead the dough and divide into 16 even-size pieces. Shape into rounds and place, well spaced, on to greased baking trays, Cover with a damp cloth and leave to prove in a warm place until double in size. Brush with beaten egg and sprinkle with coarse sugar. Bake in a pre-heated oven 375°F or Mark 5 for 20 minutes until golden. Cool on a wire rack and serve buttered.

Buttermilk Cake

4 oz. butter
4 oz. margarine
8 oz. demerara sugar
3 eggs, beaten
1 lb. flour
2 level teaspoons baking powder
2 level teaspoons bicarbonate of soda
1 level teaspoon cream of tartar
¼ level teaspoon salt
¼ level teaspoon ground ginger
1 level teaspoon grated nutmeg
12 oz. currants
4 oz. sultanas
2 oz. glacé cherries
½ pint buttermilk

Set oven to 325°F or Mark 3. Grease and line a 9 inch square cake tin. Cream the butter, margarine and sugar together in a mixing bowl. Add the eggs, the sifted dry ingredients and the buttermilk. Then stir in the currants, sultanas and cherries and mix well. Turn into the tin and bake for 1½–2 hours in the centre of the oven until the cake is firm and until a skewer inserted into the cake comes out clean. Leave in the tin to cool for about 10 minutes and turn out on to a wire rack.

If buttermilk is not available use 1 tablespoon vinegar made up to ½ pint with fresh milk.

Ginger Griddle Scones

8 oz. flour
A pinch of salt
1 level teaspoon bicarbonate of soda
1 level teaspoon ground ginger
2 oz. margarine
2 oz. caster sugar
¼ pint of milk
2 level teaspoons cream of tartar

Sift the flour, salt, bicarbonate of soda and the ginger into a mixing bowl. Rub in the fat and stir in the sugar. Dissolve the cream of tartar in the milk and use to bind the mixture to form a soft dough. Knead the dough on a lightly floured surface and divide into two portions. Form each portion into a flattened circle and cut into four. Place the 8 scones on a hot griddle or heavy based frying pan and cook for 5 minutes on each side. Serve warm with butter.

THE CUCKOO

Maids of Honour

8 oz. puff pastry
8 oz. ground almonds
4 oz. caster sugar
2 eggs, beaten
1 oz. flour
4 tablespoons double cream
Pinch ground nutmeg
2 teaspoons lemon juice
A little sifted icing sugar

Set oven to 400°F or Mark 6. Grease and flour 20 patty tins. Roll out the pastry on a lightly floured surface and use to line the tins, trimming the edges neatly. Mix together in a bowl the ground almonds and sugar, then stir in the beaten eggs, flour, cream, nutmeg and lemon juice. Divide this mixture between the pastry cases and bake for about 15 minutes or until firm and golden. Turn out on to a wire rack and allow to cool. Serve dredged with a little icing sugar.

Carrot Cake

8 oz. soft brown sugar
2 fl. oz. water
8 oz. carrot, peeled and grated
4 oz. raisins or currants
16 oz. flour
3 oz. butter
4 oz. chopped nuts
1 level teaspoon salt
1 level teaspoon bicarbonate of soda
2 level teaspoons baking powder
½ level teaspoon mixed spice
2 level teaspoons ground cinnamon

Set oven to 325°F or Mark 3. Well grease a deep 7 inch square cake tin. Put the water, sugar, raisins, carrots, spices and butter in a saucepan over a low heat until the sugar has dissolved, stirring all the time. Then boil for 3 minutes. Remove from the heat and leave until the mixture is tepid. Then stir in the sieved flour, salt, baking powder, bicarbonate of soda and nuts. Mix well together. Place in the tin and bake for about 1 hour until firm and a skewer inserted into the cake comes out clean. Leave in the tin for 15 minutes to cool and then turn out on to a wire rack. Keep for 24 hours before serving sliced and buttered. This cake keeps well.

THE BASKET WOMAN

Date and Walnut Cake

8 oz. stoned dates, chopped
1 breakfast cup boiling water
1 teaspoon bicarbonate of soda
3 oz. butter
8 oz. sugar
1 large egg, beaten
1 teaspoon vanilla essence
10 oz. flour
1 teaspoon baking powder
½ teaspoon salt

Set oven to 350°F or Mark 4. Grease and line a 12 inch x 9 inch tin. Pour the boiling water over the chopped dates and add the bicarbonate of soda. Let this stand. Meanwhile cream the butter and sugar together in a bowl. Add the beaten egg and stir in the vanilla essence. Add the flour, baking powder and salt. Add the date mixture to the cake mixture and mix well. Pour this runny mixture into the tin and bake for 40 minutes. When cool cover with icing and when set turn out or cut into slices.

ICING
2½ tablespoons demerara sugar
1 tablespoon butter
1 tablespoon single cream

Icing: Mix together the demerara sugar, butter and cream in saucepan. Bring to the boil and boil for 3 minutes, stirring constantly. Cool a little and pour over the cake. Scatter with chopped walnuts.

Digestive Biscuits

6 oz. self-raising
wholemeal flour
2 oz. fine oatmeal
1 level teaspoon salt
3 oz. butter
1 oz. soft brown sugar
4 tablespoons milk

Set oven to 375°F or Mark 5. Put the flour, oatmeal and salt into a bowl and rub in the butter until the mixture resembles breadcrumbs. Stir in the sugar and enough milk to bind to a firm dough. Roll out on a floured surface to ¼ inch thickness. Cut into 3 inch rounds and prick evenly all over with a fork. Transfer to a floured baking tray and cook for approximately 20 minutes until lightly browned. Allow to cool slightly before transferring the biscuits to a wire rack. Serve plain or buttered with cheese.

Treacle Scones

12 oz. self-raising light
wholemeal flour
3 oz. butter
1 dessertspoon black
treacle
½ teaspoon salt
7 fl. oz. milk, approx.

Set oven to 400°F or Mark 6. Add the salt to the flour in a mixing bowl and rub in the butter until the mixture resembles bread-crumbs. Stir in the treacle and enough milk to make a soft dough. Roll out gently on a floured surface to about 1–1¼ inches in thickness and cut into rounds with a 2 inch pastry cutter. Place on a greased and floured baking tray and bake at the top of the oven for 10–15 minutes. Cool on a wire tray. Serve the scones cut in half and buttered; they are delicious with lemon cheese.

Fruit and Nut Ring Cake

8 oz. butter
8 oz. caster sugar
1½ dessertspoons golden syrup
4 eggs, beaten
8 oz. flour
Pinch of salt
1 level teaspoon baking powder
1 oz. ground almonds
1½ lb. sultanas
4 oz. glacé cherries
2 oz. chopped almonds
2 oz. chopped walnuts
Grated rind of 1 lemon and 1 orange

Set oven to 325°F or Mark 3. Grease and line a 9 inch ring tin or an 8 inch round cake tin. Cream the butter, sugar and syrup in a large bowl. Add the beaten eggs and the flour, salt and baking powder and mix well. Fold in the ground almonds, then the fruit, walnuts and lemon and orange rind. Put into the tin and bake in the centre of the oven. A ring tin takes about 3 hours and a round tin about 3½ hours, with the oven being turned down to 300°F or Mark 2 after first hour. Leave to cool for 10 minutes and turn out on to a wire rack.

SPRING ON THE KENTISH DOWNS

Chocolate Tarts

½ lb. short crust pastry
4 oz. caster sugar
3 oz. ground almonds
2 oz. plain chocolate
1 egg, beaten

Set oven to 400°F or Mark 6. Grease about 20 patty pans. Roll out the pastry thinly on a floured surface and line the patty pans. Mix together thoroughly the almonds and caster sugar. Melt the chocolate in a basin over boiling water. Gradually stir the beaten egg and the melted chocolate, alternately, into the almond/caster sugar mixture. Fill the pastry cases and bake for 15 minutes.

Oaty Crumbles

4 oz. self-raising flour
½ teaspoon salt
4 oz. rolled oats
2 oz. caster sugar
1 generous tablespoon golden syrup
4 oz. butter or margarine
Oatmeal for sprinkling

Set oven to 350°F or Mark 4. Grease a 7 inch square cake tin. Melt the sugar, syrup and butter in a saucepan and remove from the heat. Sift the flour and salt into a bowl and add the oats. Pour the cooled syrup mixture on to the dry ingredients. Mix well. Press the mixture into the cake tin and sprinkle the top with oatmeal. Bake for 20 to 25 minutes until risen and light golden brown. Mark into slices, allow to cool in the tin and then turn out and break up on a wire tray.

THE APPLE ORCHARD

Vinegar Cake

8 oz. butter
1 lb. flour
8 oz. sugar
8 oz. raisins
8 oz. sultanas
8 fl. oz. milk
2 tablespoons cider vinegar
1 teaspoon bicarbonate of soda, blended with 1 tablespoon milk

Set oven to 350° F or Mark 4. Well grease and line a 9 inch cake tin. In a bowl rub the butter into the flour until the mixture resembles fine breadcrumbs and then stir in the sugar, raisins and sultanas. Pour the milk into a large jug and add the cider vinegar, then stir in the bicarbonate of soda and milk mixture (you will find it will froth up.) Add to the cake mixture and stir well. Turn into the tin and bake for 30 minutes, then reduce the oven temperature to 300°F or Mark 2 and bake for a further 1 to 1¼ hours or until a warm skewer inserted into the cake comes out clean. If the cake appears to be browning too quickly on top during cooking, cover lightly with a piece of kitchen foil. When cooked, allow the cake to cool in the tin before turning out on to a wire rack. This is a light, farmhouse fruit cake that keeps well.

Currant Pasty

½ lb. puff pastry or short-crust pastry

FILLING
1½ oz. butter
1½ oz. soft brown sugar
½ lb. currants
A few drops lemon juice
1 tablespoon rum

Set oven to 450°F or Mark 8. Roll out the pastry thinly on a floured surface into a large square (about 14 inches). Cut in half. Place half the rolled pastry on a greased baking tray. For the filling melt the butter and sugar in a saucepan. Add the rest of the ingredients and mix well. Spread the filling over the pastry to within ¼ inch of the edges and brush the edges with water. Place the other half of the pastry on top and seal the edges well. Mark into 12 squares and make a few air holes. Brush over the top lightly with milk and sprinkle with caster sugar. Bake for 20–25 minutes until golden. Transfer to a wire rack, leave to cool and when cold cut into squares.

Dundee Cake

8 oz. flour
6 oz. caster sugar
6 oz. butter or margarine
4 eggs
4 oz. currants
4 oz. raisins
4 oz. sultanas
2 oz. candied peel
1 oz. ground almonds
1 teaspoon mixed spice
1 teaspoon baking powder
½ teaspoon salt
1 oz. split, blanched almonds

Set oven to 325°F or Mark 3. Grease an 8 inch cake tin and line with greaseproof paper. Cream the fat and sugar in a bowl. Sift the flour, salt and spice together in a separate bowl. Add the eggs and the flour mixture alternately to the creamed fat, beating them in well. Add the baking powder to the last of the flour. Stir in the ground almonds. Add the fruit and peel. Gently mix. Put into the cake tin. Arrange the split almonds evenly on the top of the cake. Bake for about 2 hours or until a skewer inserted into the cake comes out clean. After the first hour, if the top is browning too quickly, cover with greaseproof paper. Allow the cake to cool slightly in the tin before turning on to a wire rack. The cake will keep for several weeks if wrapped in kitchen foil.

Farmhouse Gingerbread

10 oz. flour
2 level teaspoons ground ginger
2 level teaspoons ground cinnamon
1 level teaspoon bicarbonate of soda
4 oz. hard margarine
4 oz. soft brown sugar
6 oz. black treacle
6 oz. golden syrup
2 eggs, beaten
¼ pint boiling water

Set oven to 350°F or Mark 4. Grease and line an 8 inch square cake tin. Sift into a large bowl the flour, spices and bicarbonate of soda. Melt the margarine, sugar, syrup and treacle together in a saucepan over a slow heat, then pour this mixture into the dry ingredients. Mix well. Stir in the beaten eggs and lastly add the boiling water and stir. Pour this runny mixture into the tin and bake for 40–45 minutes until firm. Leave in the tin for about 10 minutes then turn out on to a wire rack. This cake improves in flavour if kept for 48 hours.

COTTAGE AT FARRINGFORD

Fudge Cake

½ lb. semi-sweet or digestive
biscuits (broken into small
but uneven pieces)
6 oz. chopped nuts
1 rounded tablespoon cocoa
4 oz. butter
4 oz. brown sugar
1 egg, beaten

CAKE COVERING
2 oz. plain chocolate
1 teaspoon golden syrup
½ oz. butter
1 tablespoon chopped nuts

Grease two 7 inch sandwich tins. Melt the butter in a fairly large saucepan. Add the sugar, cocoa and egg and stir them over the heat until the mixture thickens. Add the biscuits and the nuts and stir well until they are coated with the mixture. Turn into the two tins and press down evenly. Leave in a refrigerator overnight until set. Next day melt the chocolate in a basin over hot water and stir in the syrup and butter whilst the chocolate is still warm. Mix well. Use a little of the mixture to sandwich the two cakes together and spread the rest on top to decorate. Scatter the nuts on the coating before it sets.

Viennese Tartlets

8 oz. hard margarine
2 oz. icing sugar
4 oz. flour
2 oz. cornflour
1 teaspoon vanilla essence
Lemon cheese for filling

Set oven to 375°F or Mark 5. Put individual paper cases into about 18 patty tins. Cream together the fat and sugar in a bowl until really soft. Sift in the flour and cornflour and add the essence. Mix well. Place a little of the mixture in each paper case and hollow out the centre. Bake for 20 minutes. When cool dust with icing sugar and place a teaspoon of lemon cheese in each tart.

NIGHT-JAR LANE, WITLEY

Sultana Cake

1 lb. sultanas
8 oz. butter
12 oz. caster sugar
1 level teaspoon mixed spice
1 tablespoon marmalade
2 level teaspoons baking powder
Pinch of salt
3 eggs, beaten
12 oz. flour

Set oven to 325°F or Mark 3. Grease and line a round 10 inch tin. Put the fruit into a large saucepan and barely cover with cold water. Bring to the boil, and boil for 5 minutes. Drain the fruit well. Add the butter, cut up into small pieces, to the fruit in the pan. Stir until it has melted, and then mix in the marmalade. Set aside to cool. Meanwhile sift the flour, salt and spice into a large bowl. Beat the sugar and eggs together well and add to the flour mixture. Lastly add the fruit the mixture. Blend well. Pour into the tin. Bake for 1 hour then lower the temperature to 300°F or Mark 2 and bake for a further ½ hour. Leave in the tin for about 10 minutes then turn out and cool on a wire rack. This cake improves in flavour if kept for 48 hours before cutting.

Banbury Cakes

1 lb. puff pastry
2 oz. butter, melted
4 oz. raisins
4 oz. currants
2 oz. mixed peel
4 oz. demerara sugar
1 level teaspoon
mixed spice
Egg white and caster sugar
for topping

Set oven to 425°F or Mark 7. Mix the melted butter, fruit, peel, sugar and spice together in a bowl, combining well. Roll out the pastry on a lightly floured surface and, using a saucer, cut into about 16 circles. Divide the fruit mixture evenly between them, then dampen the edges of the pastry circles and draw up into the centre, sealing well. Turn over and, with the hands, gently form the cakes into ovals, then press down very gently with a rolling pin. Make 3 diagonal cuts across the top of each cake, then brush with egg white and sprinkle with sugar. Place on lightly greased baking trays and bake for 15 to 20 minutes or until golden. Serve slightly warm. Makes about 16 cakes.

Date Slices

8 oz. stoned dates
¼ pint water
1 teaspoon vanilla essence
4 oz. self-raising flour
4 oz. butter or margarine
1 level teaspoon bicarbonate of soda
4 oz. quick cooking oats
6 oz. caster sugar

Set oven to 350°F or Mark 4. Grease a shallow 7 inch x 11 inch tin. Chop the dates and place in a saucepan with the water. Bring to the boil and cook until soft. Add the essence. Sift the flour into a bowl, rub in the fat, add the bicarbonate of soda and stir in the oats and sugar. Put half the crumbly mixture in the tin and press down firmly. Cover with the dates, top with the rest of the mixture and press down. Bake for 20–30 minutes. Leave to cool in the tin and when cool, dredge with icing sugar and cut into slices.

METRIC CONVERSIONS

The weights, measurements and oven temperatures used in the preceding recipes can be easily converted to their metric equivalents.

Weights

Avoirdupois	Metric
1 oz.	just under 30 grams
4 oz. (¼ lb.)	app. 115 grams
8 oz. (½ lb.)	app. 230 grams
1 lb.	454 grams

Liquid Measures

Imperial	Metric
1 tablespoon (liquid only)	20 millilitres
1 fl. oz.	app. 30 millilitres
1 gill (¼ pt.)	app. 145 millilitres
½ pt.	app. 285 millilitres
1 pt.	app. 570 millilitres
1 qt.	app. 1.140 litres

Oven Temperatures

	°Fahrenheit	Gas Mark	°Celsius
Slow	300	2	140
	325	3	158
Moderate	350	4	177
	375	5	190
	400	6	204
Hot	425	7	214
	450	8	232
	500	9	260

Flour as specified in these recipes refers to
Plain Flour unless otherwise described